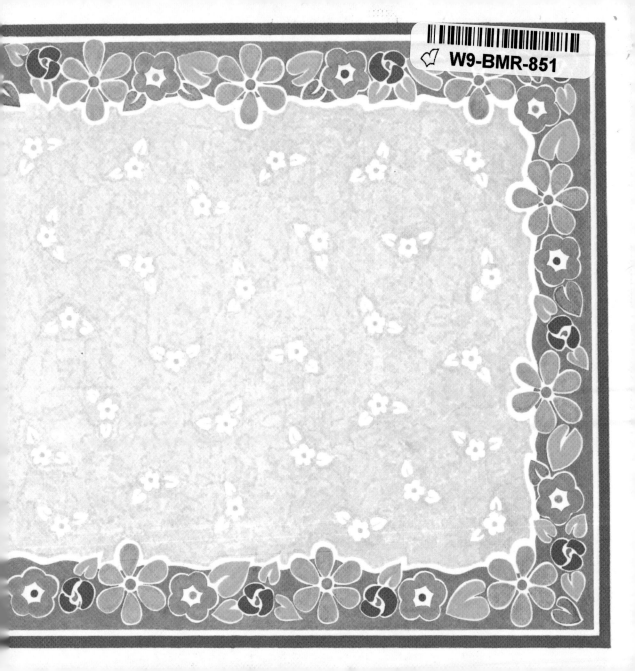

Mary Engelbreit's

Cookies

cookbook

Mary Engelbreit's
Cookies
cookbook

Illustrated by Mary Engelbreit

Photography by Alison Miksch

**Andrews McMeel
Publishing**

Kansas City

 is a registered trademark of Mary Engelbreit Enterprises, Inc.

Library of Congress Cataloging-in-Publication Data:
Engelbreit, Mary.
     Mary Engelbreit's Cookies.
          p.   cm.
     Includes index.
     ISBN 0-8362-6758-3 (hd)
     1. Cookies   I. Title.
TX772.E54   1998
641.8'654--dc21   98-22460
                                                CIP
First U.S. Edition
01 02 TWP 10 9 8 7

Editor: Deborah Mintcheff
Art Director: Nina Ovryn; Designer: Paola Pelosi
Food Stylist: Susan Ehlich; Prop Stylist: Barbara Fritz
Recipe Developers: Tracey Seaman & Judith Sutton

Produced by Smallwood & Stewart, Inc., New York City

THE MORE
THE MERRIER

 Table of Contents

Chapter One

Cookie Jar Gems

Chapter Two

Introduction

Nothing warms up a home more than the aroma of freshly baked cookies. And nothing is more delicious than a homemade cookie. If you aspire to be recognized as the Queen of your Kitchen, just put a plate of these tantalizing treats out, along with a pitcher of milk, and watch everyone come running!

I'm happy to bring you a complete collection of the best cookie recipes. These recipes are tried and true: I guarantee that each recipe is not only mouthwatering but will make you proud to serve them.

We are all so busy these days, with our time divided between so many interests and responsibilities at home and at work. Isn't it nice to have one little volume that's a complete resource for treating ourselves and our loved ones to one of our favorite indulgences? It's clear from the many letters I receive from my fans that you want recipes that taste delicious, but are easy to prepare. I think this book gives you that winning combination.

Ann Estelle and I, shown on the left in her superwoman tablecloth cape, are thrilled to bring it to you.

There are lots of ideas in here for baking with kids and I encourage you to establish this tradition with your children, whether baking for its own sake or for gift-giving or tree-trimming. It's important to show kids how much fun you can have in the kitchen, thus insuring that you are not always the only one in there.

With that in mind, I am pleased to present to you Her Majesty's Best Recipes. Enjoy!

Mary

How To Measure Ingredients

DRY INGREDIENTS: *To measure dry ingredients accurately, it is important to use standard-size dry measuring cups available in metal or plastic in sets that include 1/4-cup, 1/3-cup, 1/2-cup, and 1-cup sizes. Spoon the dry ingredient, such as flour, granulated sugar, or cocoa, into the appropriate size cup, filling it slightly above the rim. (Do not tap the cup on the counter.) Level off the top with the straight edge of a knife, using a sweeping motion.*

LIQUID INGREDIENTS: *Use a clear glass liquid measuring cup with a pouring spout available in 1-cup, 2-cup, and 4-cup sizes. Use the cup appropriate to the amount you are measuring and place on a level surface, such as the kitchen counter. Fill to the desired measure; bend down to check the accuracy of the measure at eye level. (Do not lift the cup up to read it.)*

BROWN SUGAR AND VEGETABLE SHORTENING: *Use a dry measuring cup. Firmly pack brown sugar or shortening into the cup, pressing with your fingers or a rubber spatula to eliminate any air pockets. Level off the top with the straight edge of a knife, using a sweeping motion.*

MEASURING SPOONS: *These come in graduated sets of four or more and are used to measure small amounts of both liquid and dry ingredients, ranging from 1/4 teaspoon and up to 1 tablespoon. Measure dry ingredients, such as salt, baking powder, and baking soda, by filling up the spoon and leveling off the top. Measure liquids, such as vanilla or lemon juice, by pouring them into the spoon up to the rim.*

BUTTER AND MARGARINE: *Use the measuring marks printed on the wrapper in tablespoons, ounces, and parts of a cup, using the most convenient measure. Cut off the desired amount with a small sharp knife.*

SOUR CREAM, YOGURT, AND CURD CHEESE: *Use standard dry measuring cups. Spoon the ingredients into the cup, then level off the top with the straight edge of a knife, using a sweeping motion.*

Storing Cookies

UP TO ONE WEEK:

- Soft cookies should be stored at room temperature in an air-tight container between layers of waxed paper. If they begin to harden, place a slice of apple in with the cookies.

- Crisp cookies should be stored at room temperature in a container with a loose-fitting lid, such as a cookie jar.

- Do not store hard and soft cookies together—the hard cookies will absorb the moisture from the soft cookies and lose their crispness.

- Store brownies and bar cookies at room temperature in their baking pan. Cover with foil, place in a large plastic bag, and seal.

- Meringue cookies should be stored at room temperature in an air-tight container.

- Store lemon bars and meringue-topped bars for up to several days in the refrigerator, but for the best flavor, serve at room temperature.

Freezing Cookies

MORE THAN ONE WEEK:

- Unfrosted cookies can be frozen in an air-tight container, between layers of waxed paper, for up to six months.

- Frosted cookies should be arranged on a baking sheet in a single layer and placed in the freezer until frozen. Layer the cookies between sheets of waxed paper in an air-tight container and freeze for up to two months.

- Freeze fragile cookies on a baking sheet. Place them between layers of waxed paper in an air-tight container and freeze for up to two months.

- Bar cookies can be frozen uncut. Remove from the pan, double wrap in plastic, and then wrap them in heavy foil. Freeze for up to four months.

- Zip-top freezer bags are great for freezing cookies. Be sure to remove as much air as possible from the bag, then label and date.

Cookie Jar Gems

After everyone is tucked in bed, slip into the kitchen for two or three of these cookies. Bursting with sweet chocolate chips or dusted with a rainbow of sugary sprinkles, they're homey and comforting, or—scented with cinnamon, ginger, and nutmeg—crisp and inviting. These are the reason cookie jars were invented.

Chapter One

Old-Fashioned Sugar Cookies

Here is the very best recipe for delicate, pale golden, meltingly sweet sugar cookies—every batch is a beauty. Who could say no?

Makes about 3 1/2 dozen cookies

1/2 cup (1 stick) butter,
  at room temperature

1/2 cup (1 stick) margarine,
  at room temperature

1/2 cup confectioners' sugar

1/2 cup granulated sugar

1 large egg

1 1/2 teaspoons vanilla extract

1 teaspoon baking powder

1/2 teaspoon salt

2 1/2 cups all-purpose flour

1 cup coarse white or colored
  sugar, or a combination

17

❖

1. Preheat the oven to 375°F. Lightly grease several large baking sheets.

2. In a large bowl, beat the butter, margarine, confectioners' sugar, and granulated sugar with an electric mixer until light and fluffy. Beat in the egg, vanilla, baking powder, and salt. Beat in the flour at low speed.

3. Roll pieces of the dough into 1-inch balls. Roll to coat well in the coarse sugar, then place about 2 inches apart onto the prepared baking sheets. Use the bottom of a glass to flatten each cookie into a 2-inch round. Bake for about 10 minutes, or until golden. Transfer the cookies to wire racks to cool completely.

Peanut Busters

For the men and the boys! You can increase the peanut flavor by adding chopped nuts, or toss in semisweet chocolate chips for a sweeter-tasting cookie.

Makes about 3 1/2 dozen cookies

I cup (2 sticks) unsalted butter,
   at room temperature
I 1/4 cups granulated sugar
I cup packed light brown sugar
2 large eggs
I cup natural peanut butter

2 teaspoons baking soda
1/2 teaspoon salt
3 cups all-purpose flour
I 1/2 cups mini semisweet
   chocolate chips or chopped
   peanuts (optional)

18
❖

1. Preheat the oven to 350°F.

2. In a large bowl, beat the butter, granulated sugar, and brown sugar with an electric mixer until light and fluffy. Beat in the eggs. Add the peanut butter, baking soda, and salt and beat until blended. Add the flour and mix at low speed until incorporated. Stir in the mini chips or peanuts, if using.

3. Form the dough into 1-inch balls and place 2 inches apart onto ungreased baking sheets. With the tines of a fork, gently press a crisscross pattern into the cookies, flattening them until 1/4 inch thick.

4. Bake the cookies for 14 minutes, or until golden. Let cool on the baking sheets for 2 minutes, than transfer to wire racks to cool completely.

Chocolate Chippers

*Everyone has a favorite version of this beloved classic. This is
ours—filled with chocolate chips and chopped walnuts.*

Makes about 5 dozen cookies

2 1/3 cups all-purpose flour
1 teaspoon baking soda
1/2 teaspoon salt
1 cup (2 sticks) unsalted butter,
  at room temperature
1 cup packed light brown sugar
3/4 cup granulated sugar

2 large eggs
1 1/2 teaspoons vanilla extract
1 (12-ounce) package semisweet
  chocolate chips
1 cup walnuts or pecans, coarsely
  chopped (3 1/2 ounces)

19
❖

1. Preheat the oven to 375°F.

2. In a medium bowl, whisk together the flour, baking soda, and salt.

3. In a large bowl, beat the butter and both sugars with an electric mixer until light
and fluffy. Add the eggs one at a time, beating well after each addition. Beat in the vanilla.
On low speed, gradually add the flour mixture. Using a large wooden spoon, stir in the
chocolate chips and nuts.

4. Drop the cookie dough by slightly rounded tablespoonfuls 2 inches apart onto
ungreased baking sheets.

5. Bake for 9 to 11 minutes, until the edges of the cookies are golden brown. Cool for
2 to 3 minutes on the baking sheets, then transfer to wire racks to cool completely.

Double Chocolate Chip Cookies

These are the Rolls Royce of chocolate chip cookies, spiked with big chunks
of white and semisweet chocolate and heavenly macadamia nuts.

Makes about 5 dozen cookies

2 cups all-purpose flour

1/3 cup unsweetened cocoa powder

1 teaspoon baking soda

1/4 teaspoon salt

1 cup (2 sticks) unsalted butter,
   at room temperature

1 cup granulated sugar

2/3 cup packed light brown sugar

2 large eggs

2 teaspoons vanilla extract

1 1/3 cups semisweet chocolate chips
   (8 ounces)

4 ounces white chocolate, cut into
   1/4- to 1/2-inch pieces

1 cup macadamia nuts (4 1/2 ounces),
   coarsely chopped

1. Preheat the oven to 350°F.

2. Into a medium bowl, sift together the flour, cocoa, baking soda, and salt.

3. In a large bowl, beat the butter, granulated sugar, and brown sugar with an electric mixer until light and fluffy. Add the eggs one at a time, beating well after each addition. Beat in the vanilla. On low speed, gradually add the flour mixture. Using a wooden spoon, stir in the chocolate chips, white chocolate, and nuts.

4. Drop the dough by slightly rounded tablespoonfuls 2 inches apart onto ungreased baking sheets.

5. Bake for 9 to 11 minutes, until the cookies are just set. Cool the cookies for 2 to 3 minutes on the baking sheets, then transfer to wire racks to cool completely.

Mocha Blossoms

Like a diamond in a lovely setting, a chocolate kiss crowns each of these coffee-scented crackled cookies.

Makes about 3 1/2 dozen cookies

2 cups all-purpose flour

1/2 teaspoon baking powder

1/4 teaspoon salt

1 to 1 1/2 teaspoons instant espresso powder

1 teaspoon vanilla extract

10 tablespoons (1 1/4 sticks) unsalted butter, at room temperature

3/4 cup sugar

1 large egg

About 42 chocolate kisses, unwrapped

1. Preheat the oven to 350°F.

2. In a medium bowl, whisk together the flour, baking powder, and salt. In a small dish, dissolve the espresso powder in the vanilla.

3. In a large bowl, beat the butter and sugar with an electric mixer until light and fluffy. Beat in the egg, then beat in the espresso mixture. On low speed, add the flour mixture.

4. Shape heaping teaspoonfuls of the dough into 1-inch balls and place about 2 inches apart onto ungreased baking sheets.

5. Bake the cookies for 10 to 12 minutes, until just firm to the touch. Immediately press a chocolate kiss into the center of each hot cookie; the cookies will crack slightly. Let the cookies cool for 3 to 4 minutes on the baking sheets, then carefully transfer to wire racks to cool completely.

Glazed Oatmeal Raisin Drops

A light confectioners' sugar glaze jazzes up these oatmeal gems. For a delicate citrus note, stir a little finely grated orange zest into the glaze.

Makes about 3 1/2 dozen cookies

1 1/2 cups all-purpose flour

2 teaspoons baking soda

1/4 teaspoon salt

1 cup (2 sticks) unsalted butter,
   at room temperature

1 cup packed light brown sugar

1/2 cup granulated sugar

2 large eggs

2 teaspoons vanilla extract

3 cups old-fashioned oats

1 1/2 cups raisins

GLAZE

1 cup confectioners' sugar blended
   with 2 tablespoons milk or cream

23

1. Preheat the oven to 375°F.

2. In a medium bowl, whisk together the flour, baking soda, and salt.

3. In a large bowl, beat the butter, brown sugar, and granulated sugar until light and fluffy. Beat in the eggs and vanilla. On low speed, beat in the flour mixture. Using a large wooden spoon, stir in the oats and raisins.

4. Spoon slightly rounded tablespoonfuls of the dough 2 inches apart onto ungreased baking sheets. Bake for about 14 minutes, or until golden brown. Let the cookies cool on the baking sheets for 2 minutes, then transfer to wire racks to cool completely.

5. Brush some glaze on the top of each cookie and let sit until the glaze is dry.

Ginger Krinkles

Makes about 3 dozen cookies

1/2 cup (1 stick) unsalted butter

1/4 cup unsulphured molasses

2 cups all-purpose flour

1 cup granulated sugar

1 teaspoon baking powder

1 teaspoon baking soda

2 teaspoons ground ginger

1 teaspoon ground cinnamon

1/4 teaspoon ground cloves

1/4 teaspoon grated nutmeg

2 large eggs, beaten

2 teaspoons vanilla extract

Confectioners' sugar, for coating

1. In a large saucepan, melt the butter with the molasses. Let cool.

2. In a large bowl, whisk together the flour, granulated sugar, baking powder, baking soda, ginger, cinnamon, cloves, and nutmeg.

3. Whisk the eggs and vanilla into the cooled butter mixture, then stir in the dry ingredients until blended. Cover and refrigerate for at least 2 hours, or overnight.

4. Preheat the oven to 350°F. Line baking sheets with waxed paper.

5. Roll the dough into 1-inch balls. Coat the balls generously with confectioners' sugar and set about 3 inches apart onto the prepared baking sheets. Bake for about 14 minutes, or until the cookies have puffed up and sunk and are set around the edges. Let cool on the baking sheets for 2 minutes, then transfer the cookies to wire racks to cool completely.

25

❖

Jumbo Lemon Sablés

Sablé, the French word for sand, describes this cookie's fine texture perfectly. And fresh lemon zest and juice provide a subtle citrus flavor. (photograph page 14)

Makes about 15 large cookies

2 cups all-purpose flour

1/4 teaspoon salt

3/4 cup (1 1/2 sticks) unsalted butter,
   at room temperature

1 cup confectioners' sugar

1 large egg

1 1/2 teaspoons vanilla extract

2 teaspoons grated lemon zest

LEMON GLAZE

1 tablespoon fresh lemon juice

1 cup confectioners' sugar

About 1 tablespoon cream or milk

26
❖

1. In a medium bowl, whisk together the flour and salt.

2. In a large bowl, beat the butter with an electric mixer until creamy. Add the confectioners' sugar and beat until light and fluffy. Beat in the egg, then beat in the vanilla and lemon zest. On low speed, gradually beat in the flour mixture. Cover with plastic wrap and refrigerate for about 20 minutes to firm slightly.

3. Divide the dough in half. Roll each piece of dough out between sheets of waxed paper to a 1/4-inch thickness. Leaving the dough between the sheets of paper, stack on a baking sheet and refrigerate for 20 minutes, or until firm.

4. Preheat the oven to 350°F.

5. Remove one sheet of dough from the refrigerator. Peel off the top sheet of waxed paper and replace it. Flip the dough over and remove the second sheet of paper. Using a 3 3/4- to 4-inch scalloped or plain round cutter, cut out cookies and place them 1 inch apart onto ungreased baking sheets. Repeat with the remaining dough, then gather the scraps together and reroll to make more cookies. (Chill the scraps briefly if necessary.)

6. Bake the cookies for 13 to 15 minutes, until very lightly golden around the edges. Cool for about 1 minute on the baking sheets, then transfer the cookies to wire racks to cool completely.

7. In a small bowl, using a wooden spoon, beat the lemon juice into the confectioners' sugar. Beat in just enough cream to make a smooth, spreadable glaze. Spread the glaze over the tops of the cooled cookies. Let sit for about 30 minutes, until the glaze sets completely.

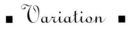

■ *Variation* ■

SUGAR-GLAZED LEMON SABLÉS: For a more classic version of this traditional cookie, omit the Lemon Glaze. Prepare the dough as directed, but increase the lemon zest to 1 tablespoon. Lightly brush the tops of the unbaked cookies with beaten egg white and sprinkle generously with coarse sugar. Bake as directed.

Cinnamon Graham Crackers

Graham flour—whole-wheat pastry flour—is available in specialty food stores.

Makes 3 dozen 2 1/2-inch squares

1 1/2 cups graham flour (see note above)

3/4 cup all-purpose flour

1/2 teaspoon baking soda

1 teaspoon cinnamon

1/2 teaspoon salt

1/4 cup (1/2 stick) unsalted butter, at room temperature

1/2 cup sugar

1 large egg

2 tablespoons maple syrup

1 tablespoon cold coffee or water

29
❖

1. Preheat the oven to 350°F.

2. In a medium bowl, whisk together the graham flour, all-purpose flour, baking soda, cinnamon, and salt. Set aside.

3. In a medium bowl, beat the butter and sugar with an electric mixer until light and fluffy. Beat in the egg, maple syrup, and coffee. On low speed, beat in the flour mixture.

4. Dust the work surface liberally with graham flour. Roll out the dough 1/8 inch thick and divide into four pieces. With a fork, score the dough (without cutting all the way through) into 2 1/2-inch squares. With a spatula, transfer the dough to ungreased baking sheets. Prick each cracker several times with a fork. Bake for 15 minutes, then transfer to wire racks to cool completely.

Currant-Cornmeal Drops

This variation on a popular Italian cookie gets its coarse texture
from cornmeal. These are great with a cup of espresso.

Makes about 6 dozen cookies

1 3/4 cups all-purpose flour

3/4 cup yellow cornmeal

1/2 teaspoon salt

1 cup (2 sticks) unsalted butter,
   at room temperature

3/4 cup plus 2 tablespoons sugar

2 large eggs

1 1/2 teaspoons vanilla extract

3/4 cup dried currants

30

1. Preheat the oven to 350°F.

2. In a medium bowl, whisk together the flour, cornmeal, and salt.

3. In a large bowl, beat the butter and sugar with an electric mixer until light and fluffy. Add the eggs one at a time, beating well after each addition. Beat in the vanilla. On low speed, gradually beat in the flour mixture. With a large wooden spoon, stir in the currants.

4. Drop the dough by generous teaspoonfuls about 1 1/2 inches apart onto ungreased baking sheets.

5. Bake the cookies for 10 to 12 minutes, until the edges are golden brown. Cool for about 2 minutes on the baking sheets, then transfer to wire racks to cool completely.

Crowd Pleasers

A platter piled with dark, chocolatey brownies; a triple-tiered dessert plate gracefully stacked with delicate meringue-topped raspberry bars; the cookie bar dream of kids (a mountain of marshmallow, brickle chips, and chocolate, crowning a rich chocolate base): these are crowd pleasers. Here are our favorite party cookies that say, "Welcome, we're glad you're here."

Chapter Two

Turtle Brownies

*Chocolate turtle candies provided the inspiration for these triple-layered confections.
Because they are so rich, offer very small portions.*

Makes 2 1/2 dozen brownies

BROWNIE LAYER
3/4 cup (1 1/2 sticks) unsalted butter
3 ounces unsweetened chocolate,
  coarsely chopped
3 large eggs
1 cup granulated sugar
1/2 cup packed light brown sugar
1 1/2 teaspoons vanilla extract
1/4 teaspoon salt
1/2 cup plus 2 tablespoons
  all-purpose flour

FILLING
36 caramels (about 10 ounces),
  unwrapped
1/2 cup heavy cream
2 1/2 cups pecans (about 10 ounces)

CHOCOLATE TOPPING
3 ounces semisweet chocolate,
  coarsely chopped
2 1/2 tablespoons heavy cream
1 teaspoon light corn syrup

1. Preheat the oven to 350°F. Grease a 13- x 9-inch baking pan.

2. In a medium saucepan, melt the butter and chocolate over low heat, stirring. Remove from the heat and let cool for about 10 minutes.

3. In a large bowl, beat the eggs and both sugars with a wooden spoon until well blended. Stir in the vanilla, then gradually beat in the chocolate mixture and the salt. Add the flour, stirring just until smooth.

4. Scrape the batter into the prepared baking pan, using a rubber spatula to spread it into the corners. Bake for 20 to 22 minutes, until the top is just firm to the touch. Transfer the pan to a wire rack.

5. Meanwhile, in a large heavy saucepan, melt the caramels with the cream over low heat, stirring frequently with a wooden spoon, until smooth. Add the pecans and stir until they are well coated with the caramel.

6. Scrape the caramel filling onto the hot brownie layer, spreading it evenly. Let cool to room temperature, then refrigerate until the filling is chilled and set.

7. In a small heavy saucepan, melt the chocolate with the cream and corn syrup, stirring until smooth. Using a fork, drizzle the chocolate topping generously over the bars in a zigzag pattern. Refrigerate briefly to set the chocolate, then, using a sharp heavy knife, cut the brownies into 30 bars. Store, covered, in the refrigerator.

Pecan-Fudge Brownies

There are countless versions of this all-American favorite, but we think this one is the best. The secret to super-fudgy brownies: underbake them.

Makes 2 dozen brownies

1 cup (2 sticks) unsalted butter

4 ounces unsweetened chocolate, coarsely chopped

4 large eggs

2 cups sugar

2 teaspoons vanilla extract

1/4 teaspoon salt

3/4 cup plus 2 tablespoons all-purpose flour

1 1/2 cups pecans or walnuts, coarsely chopped (5 1/4 ounces)

35
❖

1. Preheat the oven to 350°F. Grease a 13- x 9-inch baking pan.

2. In a medium saucepan, melt the butter and chocolate over low heat. Remove from the heat and let cool for about 10 minutes.

3. In a large bowl, mix the eggs and sugar with a wooden spoon until well blended. Add the vanilla, then gradually stir in the chocolate mixture and the salt. Gradually add the flour, mixing until smooth. Stir in the pecans.

4. Spread the batter in the prepared baking pan. Bake for 25 to 28 minutes, until the brownies are just set. (A toothpick inserted into the center will not come out clean.) Do not overbake. Set the pan on a wire rack to cool completely, then cut into 24 squares.

Rocky Road Brownies

Makes 35 brownies

1 cup (2 sticks) unsalted butter	**YUMMY BITS**
4 ounces unsweetened chocolate	1 1/2 cups miniature marshmallows
1 1/2 cups sugar	1 cup coarsely chopped walnuts
4 large eggs	1 cup almond brickle chips
1 teaspoon vanilla extract	1/2 cup sliced almonds
1/4 teaspoon salt	1/2 cup mini semisweet chocolate
1 cup all-purpose flour	chips

1. Preheat the oven to 350°F. Line a 13- x 9-inch baking pan with foil, allowing the foil to extend over the two long sides of the pan. Lightly grease the foil.

2. In a medium saucepan, melt the butter and unsweetened chocolate over low heat. Transfer to a large bowl and stir in the sugar, then beat in the eggs one at a time. Stir in the vanilla and salt, then stir in the flour.

3. In a medium bowl, toss together the ingredients for the yummy bits. Stir 3 cups of the yummy bits into the batter, then scrape the batter into the prepared pan.

4. Bake for 20 minutes. Sprinkle the remaining yummy bits over the brownies, gently pressing them into the surface. Bake for 10 minutes longer, or until the yummy bits have melted. Set the pan on a wire rack to cool completely.

5. Lift the foil and transfer the brownies to a cutting board. Cut into bars.

37
❖

Chocolate Malted Brownies

Nostalgic for the unforgettable chocolate malted of the drugstore soda fountain?
Here it is—everything but the straw.

Makes 3 dozen brownies

1/2 cup all-purpose flour

1/2 teaspoon baking powder

1/4 teaspoon salt

1/4 cup milk

1/4 cup malt powder, such as
Ovaltine

1 teaspoon vanilla extract

1/4 cup (1/2 stick) unsalted butter,
at room temperature

1 cup sugar

2 large eggs

3 ounces unsweetened chocolate,
melted and cooled

GLAZE

4 ounces milk chocolate, coarsely
chopped

1/4 cup heavy cream

2 tablespoons malt powder

1 1/2 teaspoons light corn syrup

1. Preheat the oven to 350°F. Line a 9-inch square baking pan with foil and grease the foil.

2. In a medium bowl, whisk together the flour, baking powder, and salt. In a small bowl, stir together the milk, malt powder, and vanilla. Set aside.

3. In a large bowl, beat the butter and sugar with an electric mixer until light and fluffy. Beat in the eggs. On low speed, add the flour mixture in two additions, alternating with the melted chocolate and the milk mixture. Beat until blended. Scrape the batter into the

prepared pan and smooth the top with a rubber spatula.

4. Bake for 20 to 25 minutes, until a toothpick inserted into the center comes out clean. Transfer the pan to a wire rack and let the brownies cool completely.

5. In a small saucepan, combine the chocolate, cream, malt powder, and corn syrup and heat over low heat, stirring occasionally, until smooth. Remove from the heat and let stand until thickened but still pourable.

6. Place a cutting board on top of the brownie pan, invert, remove the pan, and carefully peel away the foil. Turn the brownies right side up. Pour the glaze over and spread it evenly to cover the top. Let stand until set, then cut into 36 squares.

Golden Coconut-Lemon Bars

Adding sweetened coconut to the classic lemon topping makes these bars seem like winter in the tropics, and they're perfect with an afternoon cup of tea.

Makes 2 dozen bars

BUTTERY CRUST

1 cup (2 sticks) unsalted butter,
   at room temperature
1/2 cup confectioners' sugar
1/4 teaspoon salt
2 cups all-purpose flour

COCONUT-LEMON TOPPING

4 large eggs, at room temperature
1 1/4 cups granulated sugar
1/4 cup all-purpose flour
1/2 teaspoon baking powder
2 teaspoons grated lemon zest
1/2 cup fresh lemon juice
3 cups sweetened flaked coconut

1. Preheat the oven to 350°F. Grease a 13- x 9-inch baking pan. Line with foil, allowing the ends to extend over the two short sides of the pan. Grease the foil.

2. In a large bowl, beat the butter, confectioners' sugar, and salt with an electric mixer until light and fluffy. On low speed, gradually add the flour. Press the mixture evenly over the bottom of the pan. Bake for 14 to 16 minutes, until golden around the edges.

3. Meanwhile, in a large bowl, beat the eggs with an electric mixer until they are frothy. Beat in the granulated sugar. Beat in the flour and baking powder, then beat in the lemon

zest and juice. Add the coconut, stirring, until the topping is thoroughly mixed.

4. Scrape the topping onto the hot crust, spreading the coconut evenly. Bake for 25 to 28 minutes, until the edges are golden and the coconut is lightly browned in a few spots. Set the pan on a wire rack to cool completely. Refrigerate briefly for easier cutting.

5. Run a thin sharp knife around the sides of the pan to release the foil, if necessary. Lift up the foil by its ends and transfer the bars to a cutting board. Using a large sharp knife, cut into 24 squares. Store, well covered, in the refrigerator.

Raspberry Meringue Squares

Making a perfect meringue is not as hard as it seems, and its lighter-than-air
quality adds sophistication to this delicious confection.

Makes 2 dozen squares

BUTTERY CRUST
1 cup (2 sticks) unsalted butter,
   at room temperature
1/2 cup confectioners' sugar
1/4 teaspoon salt
2 cups all-purpose flour

MERINGUE TOPPING
3 large egg whites, at room
   temperature
1/2 cup granulated sugar

Generous 1/3 cup raspberry jam
Confectioners' sugar, for dusting

42
❖

1. Preheat the oven to 350°F. Grease a 13- x 9-inch baking pan.

2. In a medium bowl, beat the butter, confectioners' sugar, and salt with an electric mixer until light and fluffy. On low speed, gradually add the flour, beating just until incorporated; the mixture should still be somewhat crumbly. Press the mixture evenly over the bottom of the pan. Bake for 14 to 16 minutes, until lightly golden around the edges. Set the pan on a wire rack.

3. In a large bowl, beat the egg whites with an electric mixer until frothy. Increase the speed to medium-high and beat until the whites begin to form soft peaks. Add the sugar about 1 tablespoon at a time, and continue beating until the whites form stiff, glossy peaks.

4. Spread the jam evenly over the warm crust. Using a large metal spoon, drop the meringue in large dollops on the jam, and using the back of the spoon, carefully spread the meringue over the crust, making sure to seal the edges.

5. Bake for 25 minutes, or until the meringue is golden brown. (The meringue will puff up as it bakes and sink as it cools.) Set the pan on a wire rack to cool completely.

6. Using a large sharp knife, cut into 24 squares. (If necessary, run the knife under warm water and wipe dry between cuts.) Dust the tops of the bars with confectioners' sugar. Store the bars, well covered, in the refrigerator.

Cranberry-Fig Crumb Bars

In the fall, pop extra bags of fresh cranberries into your freezer so you can enjoy these at any time of the year. The oat pastry and the crumb topping are a perfect foil for the intense fig and tart cranberry flavors in this rich sweet.

Makes 5 dozen bars

CRUST AND TOPPING

2 1/4 cups all-purpose flour

1 cup packed light brown sugar

1/4 teaspoon salt

3/4 cup (1 1/2 sticks) cold unsalted
   butter, cut into small pieces

1 cup old-fashioned oats

2/3 cup finely chopped walnuts

FRUIT FILLING

1 (12-ounce) package cranberries

1 cup granulated sugar

1 1/2 cups water

1 (12-ounce) package dried Mission
   or Calmyrna figs, quartered

1 tablespoon grated orange or
   lemon zest

1/2 teaspoon ground cinnamon

44
❖

1. Preheat the oven to 350°F. Line a 15- x 10-inch jelly-roll pan with foil, allowing the foil to extend over the sides of the pan by about 2 inches.

2. In a large bowl, toss together the flour, brown sugar, and salt. Add the butter and work it in with your fingers or cut in with two knives, until the mixture resembles coarse crumbs. Add the oats and walnuts and toss to mix.

3. Set aside 1 1/3 cups of the crust mixture. Press the

remaining mixture evenly over the bottom of the prepared pan.

4. Bake for 20 to 25 minutes, until the oat pastry is lightly golden.

5. Meanwhile, in a large saucepan, combine the cranberries, granulated sugar, and water over medium-high heat and bring to a boil, stirring occasionally. Cook for 3 minutes, then stir in the figs, orange zest, and cinnamon. Reduce the heat and simmer for about 5 minutes, or until the mixture is thickened and the figs are soft. Remove the pan from the heat.

6. Scrape the filling onto the baked crust, spreading it evenly. Clump and scatter the reserved crust mixture over the fruit. Bake for 25 minutes, or until the topping is golden.

7. Set the pan on a wire rack to cool completely. Lift the bars out by the foil, then use a sharp knife lightly coated with cooking spray to cut into 60 squares.

Pecan Praline Bars

When it comes to sweets, Southerners really honor their stuff, and there the combination of pecans, brown sugar, and butter is a favorite.

Makes 5 dozen bars

BROWN SUGAR CRUST

3/4 cup (1 1/2 sticks) unsalted butter

1 cup packed dark brown sugar

2 large eggs

2 teaspoons vanilla extract

1/2 teaspoon salt

1 cup all-purpose flour

CARAMEL TOPPING

12 ounces pecans (about 3 cups)

1/2 cup (1 stick) unsalted butter

3 cups packed dark brown sugar

1/2 cup light corn syrup

1/2 teaspoon salt

1 cup heavy cream

2 tablespoons bourbon or dark rum

1. Preheat the oven to 375°F. Line a 15- x 10-inch jelly-roll pan with foil, allowing the foil to extend over the sides of the pan by about 2 inches. Grease the foil.

2. In a medium saucepan, melt the butter over medium heat. Remove from the heat and whisk in the brown sugar, then whisk in the eggs, vanilla, and salt. With a wooden spoon, stir in the flour. Scrape into the prepared pan, spreading the batter into the corners and smoothing the top with a rubber spatula. Bake for 15 minutes, or until springy to the touch. Let cool on a wire rack.

3. Meanwhile, spread the pecans on a large baking sheet and toast in the oven for 8 minutes, or until nicely golden. Set aside until completely cooled.

4. In a large saucepan, melt the butter over medium heat. Stir in the brown sugar, corn syrup, and salt. Bring to a full boil, stirring occasionally. Boil for 2 minutes, or until the caramel reaches 250°F (soft ball stage*) on a candy thermometer. Remove from the heat.

5. Carefully add the cream and bourbon to the caramel. (The mixture will bubble up.) Stir until smooth. Stir in the toasted pecans, then pour the caramel filling over the crust. Place the jelly-roll pan on a baking sheet to prevent the crust from overbrowning. Bake for 25 minutes. Carefully transfer the jelly-roll pan to a wire rack and let cool completely.

6. Place a baking sheet on top of the jelly-roll pan. Invert the pan, then remove it and peel off the foil. Cover with a large cutting board and invert it again so the bars are right side up. Using a sharp knife, cut into 60 squares.

* Soft ball stage is the point at which a drop of boiling sugar syrup immersed in cold water separates into firm but flexible threads.

Walnut Jumbles

*Sour cream in the batter gives these old-fashioned favorites
their soft, comforting texture.*

Makes about 5 dozen cookies

2 cups all-purpose flour

1 teaspoon baking powder

1/4 teaspoon baking soda

1/2 teaspoon salt

1/2 cup (1 stick) unsalted butter,
   at room temperature

1 cup sugar

1 large egg

1/4 cup sour cream

1 1/2 teaspoons vanilla extract

3/4 cup walnuts, finely chopped, plus
   1 1/4 cups walnut halves

49
❖

1. Preheat the oven to 350°F. Grease two baking sheets.

2. In a medium bowl, whisk the flour, baking powder, baking soda, and salt.

3. In a large bowl, beat the butter and sugar with an electric mixer until light and fluffy. Beat in the egg, then beat in the sour cream and vanilla. On low speed, gradually beat in the flour mixture. Beat in the chopped walnuts.

4. Drop the dough by heaping teaspoonfuls about 1 1/2 inches apart onto the prepared baking sheets. Press a walnut half into the center of each cookie, flattening the cookies slightly.

5. Bake the cookies for 12 to 14 minutes, until the edges are golden brown. Cool for 2 to 3 minutes on the baking sheets, then transfer to wire racks to cool completely.

Chocolate-Hazelnut Cookies

The combination of chocolate and hazelnuts is heavenly. For the best results, use a high-quality chocolate, such as Lindt or Ghirardelli.

Makes about 3 dozen cookies

2 cups all-purpose flour

2/3 cup hazelnuts, toasted, skinned, and very finely chopped

1 teaspoon baking powder

1/4 teaspoon salt

10 tablespoons (1 1/4 sticks) unsalted butter, at room temperature

1 cup confectioners' sugar

1 large egg

1 1/2 teaspoons vanilla extract

CHOCOLATE FILLING

6 ounces bittersweet chocolate, coarsely chopped

1/4 cup plus 2 tablespoons heavy cream

2 ounces bittersweet chocolate, melted and kept hot

1. In a medium bowl, whisk together the flour, hazelnuts, baking powder, and salt.

2. In a large bowl, beat the butter and confectioners' sugar with an electric mixer until light and fluffy. Beat in the egg, then beat in the vanilla. On low speed, gradually beat in the flour mixture. Shape the dough into a disk, wrap in plastic, and refrigerate for 1 to 2 hours, until firm enough to roll.

3. Divide the dough into quarters. Roll each piece of dough out between sheets of waxed paper to a 3/16-inch thickness. Stack the dough on a baking sheet and refrigerate

the dough for about 20 minutes, or until firm.

4. Preheat the oven to 350°F.

5. Remove one sheet of dough from the refrigerator. Peel off the top sheet of waxed paper and replace it. Flip the dough over and remove the second sheet of paper. Using a 2-inch scalloped or plain round cutter, cut out cookies and place 1 inch apart on ungreased baking sheets. Repeat with the remaining dough.

6. Bake the cookies for 10 to 12 minutes, until the edges are lightly browned. Cool for about 2 minutes on the baking sheets, then transfer to wire racks to cool completely.

7. In a food processor, process the chocolate until finely chopped. In a small saucepan, bring the cream to a boil. With the motor running, add the hot cream to the chocolate and process for about 30 seconds, or until smooth. Pour into a small bowl. Let stand for 30 minutes, or until slightly set and spreadable.

8. Spread a slightly rounded teaspoonful of the filling onto the bottom of half of the cookies. Top with the remaining cookies and gently press each sandwich together. Let the cookies sit until the filling is set.

9. To decorate the cookies, dip a fork into the melted chocolate and shake and flick it over the cookies to make a decorative zigzag pattern. Let stand until the chocolate is set.

Chocolate Mint Delights

This Oreo-like cookie is made more grown-up by its mint-flavored cream filling.
But if you crave a homemade version of the classic, leave out the mint extract.

Makes about 3 1/2 dozen cookies

COOKIE DOUGH
1 1/2 cups all-purpose flour
1/2 cup cornstarch
1/3 cup unsweetened cocoa powder
1/4 teaspoon salt
1/2 cup (1 stick) unsalted butter,
   at room temperature
3/4 cup granulated sugar
2 large eggs
2 teaspoons vanilla extract

CREAM FILLING
2 cups confectioners' sugar
1/4 cup vegetable shortening
1 tablespoon light corn syrup
1/2 teaspoon vanilla extract
1/2 teaspoon mint extract
2 drops green food color
   (optional)

53
❖

1. In a medium bowl, whisk together the flour, cornstarch, cocoa, and salt. Set aside.

2. In a large bowl, beat the butter and granulated sugar with an electric mixer until light and fluffy. Add the eggs, then the vanilla, and beat until blended. On low speed, beat in the flour mixture. Divide the dough into four pieces, shape each piece into a disk, and wrap in plastic. Refrigerate for at least 2 hours, or until firm.

3. Preheat the oven to 350°F. Lightly grease two baking sheets.

4. On a floured surface, roll out one piece of the dough at a time 1/8 inch thick. Cut out cookies with a 2-inch round (preferably fluted or scalloped) cutter. Place the cookies about 2 inches apart onto the prepared baking sheets. With a toothpick, decoratively poke holes into each cookie if desired. Bake for about 12 minutes, or until firm to the touch. Transfer the cookies to wire racks to cool completely.

5. In a large bowl, beat the confectioners' sugar, shortening, corn syrup, vanilla, mint extract, and food color, if using, with an electric mixer until smooth.

6. Spread a rounded teaspoonful of the cream filling onto the bottom of half of the cookies. Top with the remaining cookies and gently press each sandwich together.

❖

Brandy Snaps

Here you have three ways to finish these paper-thin wafers: roll and dip into chocolate, fill with brandy whipped cream, or dust with confectioners' sugar.

Makes about 28 cookies

3/4 cup plus 2 tablespoons
   all-purpose flour
1/4 teaspoon ground cinnamon
1/4 teaspoon ground ginger
Pinch of salt
1/2 cup (1 stick) unsalted butter,
   cut into 8 pieces

1/2 cup unsulphured molasses
1/2 cup sugar
2 teaspoons brandy
6 ounces white or bittersweet
   chocolate, melted and kept hot

56
❖

1. Preheat the oven to 325°F. Lightly grease two baking sheets.

2. In a medium bowl, whisk together the flour, cinnamon, ginger, and salt.

3. In a heavy medium saucepan, combine the butter, molasses, and sugar. Bring to a simmer over medium heat, stirring, until the butter melts and the mixture is smooth. Cook, stirring, for 30 seconds. Remove the pan from the heat, whisk in the flour mixture, then stir in the brandy.

4. Drop the batter by level tablespoonfuls at least 4 inches apart on the prepared baking sheets. Bake the cookies for 8 to 10 minutes, until bubbly and very slightly colored around the edges.

5. Let the cookies cool on the baking sheets for 2 minutes, or until the cookies don't

wrinkle when an edge is lifted with a metal spatula but are not yet firm. Working with one cookie at a time, place face down on a work surface and roll up around the handle of a wooden spoon. (If the cookies become too firm to roll, return them to the oven briefly.) Let the cookies set, seam side down, on a wire rack for about 30 seconds, then slide them off the spoon and place, seam side down, on wire racks to cool completely.

6. Line a work surface with waxed paper. Dip the ends of each cookie in the melted chocolate, shake off the excess, and place, seam side down, on the paper. Let sit for 1 hour, or until the chocolate is set.

■ *Variations* ■

CLASSIC FILLED BRANDY SNAPS: Make and bake the cookies as directed, but have ready several lightly greased cannoli molds or a 1-inch-thick wooden dowel. Shape the warm cookies around the molds as directed above; let cool. Prepare the filling: In a large bowl, beat 3 cups heavy cream with 3 tablespoons sugar and 1 tablespoon brandy until stiff peaks just begin to form. Fill a large pastry bag fitted with a large open star tip with the whipped cream and pipe the cream into either end of each brandy snap, filling them completely and forming a rosette at each end. Sprinkle grated bittersweet chocolate over the whipped cream. Serve, or cover and refrigerate for up to 2 hours.

MOLASSES BRANDY WAFERS: Make and bake the cookies as directed, but do not roll. Let cool on the baking sheets for 3 to 5 minutes, until firm, then transfer to wire racks to cool completely. Dust the cookies with confectioners' sugar.

Sweet

Gifts

The gift of love is treasured the most, but a gift from the kitchen is the sweetest. Here are cookies for wrapping in your gift-giving best. Tie up biscotti with lengths of raffia, layer shortbread in a hand-painted box, or arrange a constellation of meringue stars in a vintage tin. These gifts will be savored by friends and those you love.

for YOU

Chapter Three

Raspberry Linzer Hearts

Don't bring these out for the Super Bowl: they are labors of love for Valentine's Day, Mother's Day, and ladies' teas.

Makes about 4 dozen cookies

1 cup walnuts (3 1/2 ounces)

1 cup whole blanched almonds (4 ounces)

1 cup (2 sticks) unsalted butter, at room temperature

1 cup confectioners' sugar, plus additional, for dusting

2 large egg yolks

2 1/2 cups all-purpose flour

1/2 cup cornstarch

1 cup seedless raspberry or blackberry jam

60
❖

1. In a food processor, combine the walnuts and almonds and process, pulsing, until finely ground. Set aside.

2. In a large bowl, beat the butter and confectioners' sugar with an electric mixer until light and fluffy. Beat in the egg yolks. On low speed, gradually add the flour and cornstarch, mixing just until incorporated. Add the ground nuts and mix until just blended. Divide the dough into four pieces, shape each into a disk, and wrap in plastic. Refrigerate for at least 4 hours, or until firm.

3. Preheat the oven to 325°F. Grease two baking sheets.

4. On a floured surface, roll out one piece of dough at a time

until 1/4 inch thick. Using a 2 1/2-inch heart-shaped cutter, cut out as many cookies as possible. Place half of the hearts onto one of the prepared baking sheets.

5. Bake for 12 to 15 minutes, until lightly golden. Let the cookies cool slightly, then transfer to wire racks to cool completely.

6. Transfer the remaining hearts to the second baking sheet. Using a 1 1/2-inch heart-shaped cutter, cut the centers out from the hearts. Bake and cool the cutout hearts.

7. Dust the cutout hearts with confectioners' sugar. Spread a rounded teaspoon of jam onto each plain heart cookie bottom and cover with the cutout heart tops.

Black and Whites

Cardamom, an aromatic member of the ginger family, has a delicate spicy-sweet flavor that enlivens these traditional Scandinavian cookies.

Makes 3 dozen cookies

2 cups all-purpose flour

1/2 teaspoon baking powder

1/2 teaspoon ground cardamom

1/2 teaspoon salt

1 cup (2 sticks) unsalted butter,
   at room temperature

1 cup sugar

1 large egg yolk

1 teaspoon vanilla extract

6 ounces bittersweet chocolate,
   finely chopped

1 tablespoon vegetable oil

2/3 cup natural pistachios or cashews,
   finely chopped

63
❖

1. In a medium bowl, whisk together the flour, baking powder, cardamom, and salt.

2. In a large bowl, beat the butter and sugar with an electric mixer until light and fluffy. Beat in the egg yolk and vanilla. On low speed, gradually beat in the flour mixture.

3. On a floured surface, form the dough into a 14-inch log and wrap in waxed paper, twisting the ends to seal. Refrigerate for 30 minutes. Unwrap and reroll to refine the shape. Rewrap and refrigerate for at least 3 hours, or overnight.

4. Preheat the oven to 375°F.

5. Using a sharp knife, cut the dough into 1/4-inch slices and place 1 inch apart onto ungreased baking sheets. Bake for about 10 minutes, or until golden. Transfer the cookies to wire racks to cool completely.

6. In a small saucepan, melt half the chocolate over low heat. Remove from the heat and add the remaining chocolate and the oil, stirring occasionally, until smooth. Scrape into a small bowl. Dip each cookie halfway into the chocolate, sprinkle pistachios over the chocolate, and place the cookies on wire racks until the chocolate sets.

■ *Variations* ■

POLAR BEARS: Make the dough and stir in 2 ounces unsweetened chocolate, melted and cooled. Roll, chill, slice, and bake as directed. Substitute 6 ounces white chocolate for the bittersweet and sprinkle with 1/2 cup chopped peppermint candy instead of the nuts. Decorate as directed.

PINWHEELS: Make the dough and divide it in half. Flatten one piece of the dough and drizzle with 1 ounce unsweetened chocolate, melted and knead it in. Shape each piece of dough into a 6-inch square, wrap in waxed paper, and refrigerate for 1 hour, or until firm. Roll out the plain dough between 2 sheets of waxed paper to a 14- x 7-inch rectangle. Remove the top sheet of paper. Roll out the chocolate dough to a 14- x 7-inch rectangle and place on top of the vanilla dough, gently pressing the two doughs together. Beginning with a long side, use the paper to help lift the dough and roll it up into a tight cylinder. Wrap in waxed paper and chill. Slice and bake as directed.

Chocolate Almond Dunkers

*Sturdy little travellers, dunkers make a cup of coffee at work a memorable treat.
They're equally delicious with fresh, cold milk.*

Makes 4 dozen cookies

1 1/2 cups whole natural almonds
  (6 ounces)
4 ounces unsweetened chocolate,
  chopped
3 tablespoons unsalted butter
2 cups all-purpose flour
1 cup sugar

2 teaspoons baking powder
1/4 teaspoon salt
3 large eggs
1 tablespoon vanilla extract
8 ounces bittersweet chocolate,
  finely chopped

65
⁘

1. Preheat the oven to 350°F.

2. Place the almonds on a baking sheet and bake for about 8 minutes, or until lightly toasted. Let cool completely, then coarsely chop in a food processor. Set aside.

3. In a small saucepan, melt the unsweetened chocolate and butter over low heat. Remove from the heat and let cool.

4. In the food processor, combine the flour, sugar, baking powder, and salt, processing until combined. Add the eggs, vanilla, and the melted chocolate mixture, processing until just combined. On a work surface, knead the dough until it is shiny, then knead in the nuts, flouring your hands as needed. Divide the dough into four equal pieces. Wrap in waxed paper and refrigerate for 1 hour, or until firm.

5. Roll each piece of dough into a 9-inch log and place at least 2 inches apart on two ungreased baking sheets. Using your fingers, gently press on the logs until they are about 1 1/2 inches wide.

6. Bake for 25 minutes, or until partially set but not firm. With a spatula, very carefully transfer the baked strips to wire racks and let cool for 10 to 15 minutes. Transfer the strips to a cutting board and using a sharp serrated knife, cut each strip into 1/2-inch slices. Place the slices, cut side down, on the baking sheets and bake for 8 minutes, or until firm. Transfer the slices to wire racks to cool completely.

7. In a small saucepan, melt half the bittersweet chocolate over low heat. Remove from the heat and add the remaining bittersweet chocolate, stirring until smooth. Transfer the chocolate to a shallow bowl. Holding each biscuit level, dip the top half of each cookie into the chocolate, letting any excess drip off. Stand the cookies right side up on a sheet of waxed paper; let sit until the chocolate is set.

Buttery Spritz Cookies

*These are just about the simplest cookies you can make, and they can be
dressed up in countless ways for gift-giving.*

Makes about 7 dozen cookies

1 cup (2 sticks) unsalted butter,
   at room temperature
1 cup granulated sugar
1 large egg
1 tablespoon vanilla extract or
   1 teaspoon almond extract

1/2 teaspoon salt
2 1/2 cups all-purpose flour

DECORATION
Red and green sugar
Multicolored sprinkles
Glacé fruit

69
❖

1. Preheat the oven to 350°F.

2. In a large bowl, beat the butter and granulated sugar with an electric
mixer until light and fluffy, about 5 minutes. Add the egg, vanilla, and salt
and beat until blended. On low speed, gradually beat in the flour.

3. Following the manufacturer's instructions, place the dough into a
cookie press and press cookies about 2 inches apart onto ungreased
baking sheets. Decorate the cookies with colored sugar, multicolored
sprinkles, and/or glacé fruit.

4. Bake for 10 to 12 minutes, until golden. Transfer the cookies to
wire racks to cool completely.

Classic Shortbread

There is nothing like homemade shortbread—so buttery it just about melts in your mouth.

Makes 3 dozen cookies

1 cup (2 sticks) unsalted butter, at room temperature	1 1/2 teaspoons vanilla extract
	1/4 teaspoon salt
2/3 cup confectioners' sugar, sifted	2 cups all-purpose flour

1. In a large bowl, beat the butter and sugar with an electric mixer until light and fluffy. Beat in the vanilla and salt. On low speed, gradually beat in the flour.

2. Divide the dough into three pieces. Shape each piece into a disk, wrap in plastic, and refrigerate for 45 minutes, or until firm enough to roll.

3. Preheat the oven to 325°F.

4. Place one piece of dough between two sheets of plastic wrap. Roll out to an 8-inch round, lightly flouring the bottom sheet of plastic and the top of the dough as necessary. Remove the top piece of plastic, invert the dough onto one end of a large baking sheet, and peel off the plastic.

5. Using a long sharp knife, cut the dough into 12 wedges, but do not separate the wedges. Crimp the dough by pressing the tines of a fork around the edge, then prick all over in a decorative pattern. Repeat with the remaining pieces of dough, placing the second round on the first baking sheet and the third round in the center of another baking sheet.

6. Bake for 15 minutes, or until the edges of the shortbread are lightly golden and the centers are set. Let cool for 1 minute. Using a sharp knife, cut the shortbread along the scored lines into wedges. Let the shortbread cool for 2 to 3 minutes longer on the baking sheets, then transfer to wire racks to cool completely.

■ *Variations* ■

CHOCOLATE-DIPPED FINGERS: Prepare the dough as directed, but divide in half. Shape each half into a 7- x 4-inch rectangle; chill until firm. Roll out each piece of dough between sheets of plastic wrap to a 10- x 6 1/2-inch rectangle. Peel off the top sheet of plastic and trim the edges even. Cut the dough lengthwise into four strips, then cut each strip crosswise into five pieces. Place 1 inch apart on ungreased baking sheets. (The scraps can be rerolled.) Bake for 12 to 15 minutes, until golden brown on the bottom. Cool for 2 minutes, then transfer to wire racks to cool completely. Line a work surface with waxed paper. Melt 6 ounces bittersweet chocolate. Dip the cookies into the chocolate, coating the bottom third. Shake off the excess chocolate and place the cookies on the waxed paper. Let stand for about 1 hour, or until the chocolate is set.

72
❖

LEMON–POPPY SEED SHORTBREAD: Make the dough as directed, but reduce the vanilla to 1 teaspoon and add 1 tablespoon poppy seeds and 2 teaspoons grated lemon zest. Shape level tablespoonfuls of the dough into balls and place 2 inches apart onto ungreased baking sheets. Using the bottom of a glass, flatten each cookie to a generous 1/4-inch thickness, dipping the bottom of the glass in flour as needed to prevent sticking. Bake for 12 to 15 minutes, until golden brown on the bottom. Cool the cookies for 1 to 2 minutes, then transfer to wire racks to cool completely. To decorate the cookies: In a small bowl, stir together 1/2 cup confectioners' sugar, 1 1/2 teaspoons fresh lemon juice, and 1 tablespoon milk, or just enough to make a smooth glaze. Using a fork, drizzle the glaze over the cookies. Let stand until the icing sets.

Orange-Cardamom Biscotti

These twice-baked cookies are richly flavored with candied orange and almonds.

Makes about 4 dozen cookies

2 1/4 cups all-purpose flour

1/2 teaspoon baking powder

1/2 teaspoon baking soda

1 teaspoon ground cardamom

1/4 teaspoon salt

3 large eggs

1 cup sugar

1 teaspoon vanilla extract

1 tablespoon grated orange zest

1 1/4 cups slivered almonds (about
      5 ounces)

2/3 cup candied orange peel, chopped

1. Preheat the oven to 300°F. Grease and flour a large baking sheet.

2. In a large bowl, whisk the flour, baking powder, baking soda, cardamom, and salt.

3. In a medium bowl, beat the eggs and sugar with a wooden spoon. Add the vanilla and orange zest, then stir into the flour mixture. Stir in the almonds and candied peel.

4. Spoon the dough onto the prepared baking sheet, forming two strips 13 inches long and 2 1/4 inches wide, placing them 3 1/2 inches apart. With wet fingertips, smooth the tops and sides of the strips (they don't have to be perfect).

5. Bake for 40 minutes, or until golden. Set the baking sheet on a wire rack and cool for 5 minutes. Reduce the oven temperature to 275°F.

6. Using a sharp serrated knife, cut each strip on the diagonal into 1/2-inch slices. Stand the slices 1/2 inch apart on the baking sheet. Bake for 20 minutes, or until lightly toasted. Set on a wire rack to cool completely.

73
❖

Cranberry-Pistachio Biscotti

Golden raisins make a tasty alternative for the cranberries in this crunchy cookie.

Makes about 4 dozen cookies

2 1/4 cups all-purpose flour

1/2 teaspoon baking powder

1/2 teaspoon baking soda

1/4 teaspoon salt

3 large eggs

1 cup sugar

1 1/2 teaspoons vanilla extract

1 1/4 cups unsalted pistachios,
chopped (about 5 1/2 ounces)

3/4 cup dried cranberries, chopped

1. Preheat the oven to 300°F. Grease and flour a large baking sheet.

2. In a large bowl, whisk together the flour, baking powder, baking soda, and salt.

3. In a medium bowl, beat the eggs and sugar together with a large wooden spoon until blended. Beat in the vanilla. Add the egg mixture to the flour mixture and stir until thoroughly blended. Stir in the pistachios and cranberries.

4. Spoon the dough onto the prepared baking sheet, forming two strips about 13 inches long and 2 1/4 inches wide, placing them 3 1/2 inches apart. With wet fingertips, smooth the tops and sides of the strips (they don't have to be perfect).

5. Bake for 40 minutes, or until golden and firm to the touch. Set the baking sheet on a wire rack to cool for 5 minutes. Reduce the oven temperature to 275°F.

6. Using a sharp serrated knife, cut each strip on the diagonal into 1/2-inch slices. Stand the slices 1/2 inch apart on the baking sheet. Bake for 20 to 25 minutes, until lightly toasted. Set the baking sheet on a wire rack to cool completely.

Mexican Wedding Cakes

The unassuming appearance of these sandy-textured cookies belies their scrumptious taste. Be sure to dust them generously with confectioners' sugar.

Makes about 2 1/2 dozen cookies

1 cup pecans or walnuts (about 4 ounces)

2 cups all-purpose flour

1 cup (2 sticks) unsalted butter, at room temperature

1/2 cup confectioners' sugar, plus additional sifted confectioners' sugar, for coating

2 teaspoons vanilla extract

1. Preheat the oven to 325°F.

2. Spread the nuts on a baking sheet and toast for 10 minutes, or until lightly golden. Let the nuts cool, then finely chop.

3. In a medium bowl, toss the flour with the nuts; set aside.

4. In a large bowl, beat the butter and confectioners' sugar with an electric mixer until light and fluffy. Beat in the vanilla. On low speed, gradually add the flour mixture.

5. Roll tablespoonfuls of the dough into 1-inch balls and place 2 inches apart onto ungreased baking sheets. Bake for 16 minutes, or until lightly colored. Let the cookies cool on the baking sheets for 2 minutes, then roll while warm in confectioners' sugar. Place the cookies on wire racks to cool completely, then generously roll the cookies again in confectioners' sugar.

Almond Crescents

Grown-ups and kids alike will enjoy shaping these cookies, and enjoy eating them even more.

Makes about 5 dozen cookies

1 cup slivered almonds (about 4 ounces)

3/4 cup plus 2 tablespoons confectioners' sugar plus additional sifted confectioners' sugar, for coating

1 cup (2 sticks) unsalted butter, at room temperature

1 teaspoon vanilla extract

Pinch of salt

2 cups all-purpose flour

1. Preheat the oven to 350°F.

2. In a food processor, combine the almonds and 2 tablespoons of the confectioners' sugar and process until the almonds are finely ground.

3. In a large bowl, beat the butter and the remaining 3/4 cup confectioners' sugar with an electric mixer until light and fluffy. Beat in the vanilla. On low speed, beat in the salt, then gradually beat in the flour. Beat in the ground almond mixture.

4. Shape heaping teaspoonfuls of the dough into 2-inch crescents and place about 2 inches apart onto ungreased baking sheets.

5. Bake the cookies for 12 to 15 minutes, until lightly golden on the bottom. Cool for 2 to 3 minutes on the baking sheets, then generously coat the warm cookies with confectioners' sugar. Transfer to wire racks to cool completely.

77

sweet for you gifts

Meringue Clouds

*Make these ethereal cookies on a day with low humidity—they'll bake
up light and crisp.*

Makes about 1 1/2 dozen cookies

3 large egg whites, at room
    temperature
Pinch of salt

3/4 cup superfine sugar
2 ounces bittersweet chocolate,
    melted and cooled slightly

1. Preheat the oven to 225°F. Line two large baking sheets with parchment paper or foil.

2. In a large bowl, beat the egg whites with an electric mixer until frothy. Add the salt, increase the speed to medium-high, and beat until the whites begin to form soft peaks. Add the sugar about 1 tablespoon at a time and continue beating until stiff peaks form.

3. Spoon about half the meringue into a large pastry bag fitted with a large star tip. Pipe 1 1/2-inch rosettes about 1 inch apart onto the prepared baking sheets. Repeat with the remaining meringue.

4. Bake for 1 1/4 to 1 1/2 hours, until the meringues are firm to the touch and barely beginning to color. Set the baking sheets on wire racks to cool completely.

5. To fill the cookies, using a pastry brush, brush a thin layer of the melted chocolate over the bottom of one meringue. Place a second meringue, flat side down, against the chocolate, and press together gently to make a sandwich. Place on waxed paper or a plate

78
❖

and repeat with the remaining meringues. Let sit for 15 to 30 minutes, until the chocolate is set. Store the meringues in a dry place in an airtight container.

■ Variations ■

CHOCOLATE MERINGUE STARS: Line two large baking sheets with sheets of parchment paper or foil. Using a 2 3/4- to 3-inch star cookie cutter as a guide, trace 7 to 8 stars about 1 inch apart on each sheet of parchment. Place the paper tracing side down. (If using foil, place the foil on the baking sheets and use a toothpick to trace the stars.) Sift together 2 tablespoons of the superfine sugar and 2 tablespoons unsweetened cocoa powder; set aside. Prepare the meringue as directed, using the remaining 1/2 cup plus 2 tablespoons sugar. When the whites have formed stiff glossy peaks, sift the cocoa mixture over them and gently fold in with a large rubber spatula. Spoon the meringue about half at a time, into a large pastry bag fitted with a large star tip, and following the guidelines, pipe stars onto the baking sheets. Bake for 1 to 1 1/4 hours, until the meringues are firm to the touch. Makes about 15 stars.

CHOCOLATE CHIP MERINGUE DROPS: Prepare the meringue as directed, then gently fold in 1/2 cup mini semisweet chocolate chips. Drop the meringue by generous teaspoonfuls about 1 inch apart onto the lined baking sheets. Bake for 1 to 1 1/4 hours, until the meringues are firm to the touch and are just barely beginning to color. Makes about 4 dozen meringues.

Kids' Cookies

Christmas mice, squiggly caterpillars, peppermint candy canes—that's what baking with kids is all about. Twist ribbons of dough to shape holiday wreaths, see whose thumb makes the best jam holder for thumbprint cookies, or roll a batch of sugarplums in sugar till they shimmer. You'll be the envy of every sugarplum fairy.

Chapter Four

Twisters

Bring the spirit of the Christmas season alive by helping little hands shape this dough into candy canes, wreaths, and chocolate-sprinkled pretzels.

Makes about 4 dozen cookies

I cup (2 sticks) unsalted butter, at room temperature
3/4 cup sugar
2 large egg yolks

I 1/2 teaspoons vanilla extract
1/4 teaspoon salt
2 1/4 cups all-purpose flour
Chocolate sprinkles, for decoration

1. In a large bowl, beat the butter and sugar with an electric mixer until light and fluffy. Add the egg yolks, vanilla, and salt and beat until combined. On low speed, gradually beat in the flour. Cover the bowl with plastic wrap and refrigerate for at least 2 hours, or until the dough is firm.

2. Preheat the oven to 350°F.

3. Place the sprinkles on a sheet of waxed paper. On a work surface, using your palms, roll a heaping tablespoonful of dough into a 6-inch rope. Twist the rope into a pretzel shape, then place on top of the sprinkles, gently pressing them in. Repeat with the remaining dough, placing the pretzels, sprinkle side up, 1 inch apart, onto ungreased baking sheets.

4. Bake for 10 minutes, or until lightly colored. Let cool for about 2 minutes on the baking sheets, then transfer to wire racks to cool completely.

■ *Variations* ■

CANDY CANES: Omit the chocolate sprinkles and make the dough as directed, but divide it in half. Mix 1/2 teaspoon red food color and 1/4 cup chopped peppermint candies into one half. Cover and refrigerate as directed. For each cookie, roll 1 tablespoon of each dough into a 4-inch rope. Twist the two ropes together and curve into a candy cane shape. Bake as directed.

HOLIDAY WREATHS: Omit the chocolate sprinkles and make the dough as directed, but divide it in half. Mix 1/2 teaspoon red food color into one half and 1/2 teaspoon green food color into the other half. Cover and refrigerate as directed. For each cookie, roll 1 tablespoonful of each dough into a 4-inch rope. Twist the two ropes together, form into a wreath, and press the ends together. Decorate with silver and gold dragées. Bake as directed.

Crazy Caterpillars

Makes about 2 dozen cookies

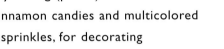

2 cups all-purpose flour

1/2 teaspoon baking powder

1/4 teaspoon salt

1/2 cup (1 stick) unsalted butter,
   at room temperature

3/4 cup plus 2 tablespoons sugar

1 large egg

1 teaspoon vanilla extract

Royal Icing (p. 103)

Cinnamon candies and multicolored
   sprinkles, for decorating

1. In a medium bowl, whisk together the flour, baking powder, and salt. Set aside.

2. In a large bowl, beat the butter and sugar with an electric mixer until light and fluffy. Beat in the egg and vanilla. On low speed, beat in the flour mixture. Divide the dough in half, shape into two disks, and wrap in plastic. Refrigerate for 2 hours, or until firm.

3. Preheat the oven to 350°F.

4. On a floured work surface, roll out one piece of the dough at a time until 1/4 inch thick. Using a 1 1/2-inch biscuit cutter, cut out as many dough rounds as possible. On ungreased baking sheets, form caterpillars by placing four dough rounds in a row for each caterpillar, overlapping them by one third, and place the caterpillars 2 inches apart.

5. Bake for about 10 minutes, or until they begin to brown around the edges. Let the cookies cool for 2 minutes on the baking sheets, then transfer to wire racks to cool.

6. Drizzle the royal icing over the cookies and decorate with cinnamon candies and sprinkles as desired. Let stand until the icing sets.

85
❖

Chocolate Crackles

These rich, fudgy cookies develop a cracked surface during baking. For a more dramatic look, coat them generously with the confectioners' sugar.

Makes about 3 1/2 dozen cookies

1 1/2 cups all-purpose flour
1/2 teaspoon baking powder
1/8 teaspoon salt
10 tablespoons (1 1/4 sticks) unsalted
   butter, at room temperature
3/4 cup granulated sugar

1 large egg
1 teaspoon vanilla extract
6 ounces bittersweet chocolate,
   melted and cooled slightly
Sifted confectioners' sugar, for
   coating

87

❖❖

1. Preheat the oven to 350°F. Lightly grease two baking sheets.

2. In a medium bowl, whisk together the flour, baking powder, and salt.

3. In a large bowl, beat the butter and granulated sugar with an electric mixer until light and fluffy. Beat in the egg, then beat in the vanilla. Gradually add the melted chocolate, mixing until blended. On low speed, beat in the flour mixture.

4. Shape level tablespoonfuls of the dough into balls and place the balls 2 inches apart onto the prepared baking sheets. As you fill each baking sheet, roll the balls generously in confectioners' sugar.

5. Bake the cookies for 10 to 12 minutes, until the tops are cracked and the cookies are just set. Cool for 1 to 2 minutes on the baking sheets, then transfer to wire racks to cool completely.

Munchable Mice

Shape these adorable mice into various sizes and create an entire mouse family.

Makes about 3 dozen cookies

1 cup (2 sticks) unsalted butter,
  at room temperature
1 cup packed light brown sugar
1 large egg
1 tablespoon vanilla extract
3 cups all-purpose flour

1/2 cup unsweetened cocoa powder

DECORATION
Unsalted peanuts
Currants
Black shoestring licorice, cut into
  3-inch lengths

1. Preheat the oven to 325°F.

2. In a large bowl, beat the butter and sugar with an electric mixer until light and fluffy. Beat in the egg and vanilla. On low speed, gradually beat in 2 1/2 cups of the flour.

3. Divide the dough in half. On a work surface, knead the remaining 1/2 cup flour into one piece of the dough. Knead the cocoa into the other piece.

4. For each mouse, pull off a piece of dough and roll the dough into a 1 1/4-inch ball. Taper at one end to form a teardrop shape. With a toothpick, make a 1-inch-deep hole in the rounded end for the tail. At the narrow end, insert 2 peanut halves for ears and 2 currants for eyes. Place the mice about 2 inches apart onto ungreased baking sheets.

5. Bake for 18 minutes, or until golden on the bottom. Transfer the cookies to wire racks and carefully insert the licorice tails. Let cool completely.

89

Walnut Thumbprints

Makes about 3 1/2 dozen cookies

2 cups all-purpose flour

1/2 teaspoon baking powder

1/4 teaspoon salt

10 tablespoons (1 1/4 sticks) unsalted
   butter, at room temperature

1/2 cup granulated sugar

1/4 cup packed light brown sugar

1 large egg

1 teaspoon vanilla extract

1 cup walnuts finely chopped

About 2/3 cup raspberry jam or
   about 42 chocolate kisses,
   unwrapped

91
❖

1. Preheat the oven to 350°F.

2. In a medium bowl, whisk together the flour, baking powder, and salt.

3. In a large bowl, beat the butter and both sugars with an electric mixer until light and fluffy. Beat in the egg and vanilla. On low speed, gradually add the flour mixture.

4. Put the walnuts in a shallow bowl. Shape heaping teaspoonfuls of the dough into 1-inch balls and roll in the walnuts, pressing to coat. Place about 2 inches apart onto ungreased baking sheets, and with your thumb, make a deep depression in the center of each cookie. If using jam, spoon 1/2 teaspoon into each hollow.

5. Bake for 10 minutes, or until golden around the edges. If using chocolate kisses, immediately press a kiss into each hot cookie. Cool the cookies for 3 minutes on the baking sheets, then transfer to wire racks to cool completely.

Sugarplums

Sugarplums, not a true cookie since they don't contain flour, are nonetheless a festive addition to any holiday table.

Makes about 2 dozen confections

I cup pitted dates

1/2 cup dried figs or pitted prunes

1/2 cup pecans

1/3 cup candied orange peel

I cup sweetened flaked coconut

I teaspoon orange juice or water

Superfine sugar, for coating

92

❖

1. In a food processor, combine the dates, figs, pecans, and candied peel. Process until chopped. Add the coconut and orange juice and process, pulsing, until the mixture begins to clump.

2. Turn the mixture out onto a sheet of waxed paper and shape into scant 1-inch balls.

3. Place the superfine sugar in a shallow bowl and roll the balls in the sugar, coating them well. Store in an airtight container for up to 3 days.

Dog Bone Cookies

Makes about 5 1/2 dozen cookies

2 cups all-purpose flour

1 teaspoon baking powder

1/4 teaspoon salt

10 tablespoons (1 1/4 sticks) unsalted
   butter, at room temperature

1 cup packed dark brown sugar

1 large egg

1 1/2 teaspoons vanilla extract

ICING

1 cup confectioners' sugar

Green or red food color

1. In a medium bowl, whisk together the flour, baking powder, and salt.

2. In a large bowl, beat the butter and brown sugar with an electric mixer until light and fluffy. Beat in the egg, then beat in the vanilla. On low speed, gradually beat in the flour mixture. Divide the dough into four pieces, shape each piece into a disk, and wrap in plastic. Refrigerate for about 2 hours, or until the dough is firm enough to roll.

3. Preheat the oven to 350°F.

4. On a lightly floured surface, roll out the dough 3/16 inch thick. Cut out cookies using a bone-shaped cutter and place 1 1/2 inches apart onto ungreased baking sheets. Bake for 8 to 10 minutes, until the edges are very lightly browned. Cool for about 2 minutes on the baking sheets, then transfer to wire racks to cool completely.

5. In a small bowl, combine the confectioners' sugar with enough water to make a smooth icing. Tint the icing with food color and pipe a name onto each cookie. Let the cookies stand until the icing is set.

93
∴

PB and J's

Make these cookies ahead, but fill them no more than twenty four hours in advance.

Makes about 5 1/2 dozen cookies

2 cups all-purpose flour	1 1/3 cups sugar
1 teaspoon baking soda	3/4 cup smooth peanut butter
1/4 teaspoon salt	1 large egg
3/4 cup (1 1/2 sticks) unsalted butter,	1 teaspoon vanilla extract
at room temperature	About 2/3 cup seedless raspberry jam

94
❖

1. In a medium bowl, whisk together the flour, baking soda, and salt.

2. In a large bowl, beat the butter and sugar with an electric mixer until light and fluffy. Beat in the peanut butter. Beat in the egg, then beat in the vanilla. On low speed, gradually beat in the flour mixture, beating just until blended.

3. Divide the dough into four pieces. Place each piece on a sheet of plastic wrap and shape into 4-inch logs about 1 3/4 inches in diameter. Wrap the logs in the plastic and twist the ends to seal. Place in the freezer for 30 to 45 minutes, until firm.

4. Reroll each log into a smooth cylinder. Wrap and freeze for 2 hours, or until firm.

5. Preheat the oven to 350°F. Cut the logs into 3/16-inch slices and place 1 inch apart onto ungreased baking sheets. Bake for 10 minutes, or until the edges are very lightly browned. Cool for 2 minutes, then transfer to wire racks to cool completely.

6. Spread a scant teaspoon of preserves onto the bottom of half the cookies. Top with the remaining cookies and gently press each sandwich together.

Holiday Treats

The living room is alive with the scent of freshly cut evergreens. Favorite ornaments brought down from the attic have been set out, ready to decorate the tree. This is the time to make the holidays truly special, with buttery bells aglow with brightly colored sugar, gingerbread kids piped with icing, and glittery cinnamon-sugar stars. Let the joyous season begin!

Chapter Five

Sugar Cookie Cutouts

This butter dough is especially easy to work into any shape. Since time is precious during the holidays, prepare the dough ahead and freeze for up to three months.

Makes about 3 1/2 dozen cookies

3 cups all-purpose flour

1 teaspoon baking soda

1/2 teaspoon salt

1 cup (2 sticks) unsalted butter,
   at room temperature

1 cup sugar

2 large eggs

2 teaspoons vanilla extract

Colored sugar and multicolored
   sprinkles, for decorating

1. In a medium bowl, whisk together the flour, baking soda, and salt.

2. In a large bowl, beat the butter and sugar with an electric mixer until light and fluffy. Beat in the eggs, then the vanilla. On low speed, gradually beat in the flour mixture.

3. Divide the dough into thirds, shape each piece into a disk, and wrap in plastic. Refrigerate for at least 2 hours, or overnight.

4. Preheat the oven to 350°F.

5. On a lightly floured surface, roll out the dough 1/8 inch thick. Cut out Christmas shapes with cookie cutters and place 2 inches apart onto ungreased baking sheets. Decorate with colored sugar and sprinkles.

6. Bake for 10 minutes, or until the edges begin to brown. Use a skewer to make a hole large enough for a ribbon to fit through. Let the cookies cool on the baking sheets for 2 minutes, then transfer to wire racks to cool completely.

Polka Dot Cows

Don't stop at cows. Make a whole farm of whimsical polka dot animals.

Makes about 4 dozen cookies

4 cups all-purpose flour

2 teaspoons baking powder

1/2 teaspoon salt

1 cup plus 2 tablespoons
  (2 1/4 sticks) unsalted butter,
  at room temperature

1 3/4 cups sugar

2 large eggs

1 tablespoon vanilla extract

1/3 cup unsweetened cocoa powder,
  sifted

Coarse sugar or granulated sugar,
  for sprinkling

1. In a medium bowl, whisk together 3 2/3 cups of the flour, the baking powder, and salt.

2. In a large bowl, beat the butter and sugar with an electric mixer until light and fluffy. Beat in the eggs, then beat in the vanilla. On low speed, gradually beat in the flour mixture. Transfer half of the dough to a medium bowl. Beat the remaining 1/3 cup flour into half the dough, then beat the cocoa into the other half. Shape the dough into two disks, wrap in plastic, and refrigerate for 2 hours, or until firm enough to roll.

3. Preheat the oven to 350°F. Lightly grease two baking sheets.

4. On a lightly floured surface, roll out half of the plain dough 1/4 inch thick. Using a 4-inch cow-shaped cutter, cut out enough

99

❖

cookies to fill the remaining baking sheet. (If the kitchen is warm, refrigerate the first sheet of cookies while you roll out the second.) Using very small round cutters, such as the wide ends of pastry tips (1/4- to 3/4-inch), cut out rounds of dough from the plain cows, setting the rounds next to the cows as you cut them. Then cut a matching number of rounds from the chocolate cows. Fit the chocolate rounds into the plain cows and the plain rounds into the chocolate cows. Sprinkle with sugar. If desired, use a skewer to make a 1/4-inch hole in the top of each cookie.

5. Bake the cookies for 8 to 10 minutes, until the edges are very lightly browned. Cool for about 1 minute on the baking sheets, then transfer to wire racks to cool completely. Repeat with the remaining dough.

■ *Variation* ■

POLKA DOT PIGS: Increase the flour to 4 1/3 cups and omit the cocoa. Prepare the dough as directed, but combine all the flour with the baking powder and salt. Add all the flour mixture to the dough, then divide it in half. Knead enough red food color into one half of the dough to tint it pale pink. Wrap the dough in plastic and refrigerate. Using a 2 3/4-inch pig-shaped cutter, cut out and bake cookies as directed above. Makes about 7 1/2 dozen cookies.

Gingerbread Kids

*Spiced cookies are always a favorite during the holidays and these are classics—
crisp and with a rich ginger flavor enhanced by molasses.*

Makes about 3 dozen cookies

2 cups all-purpose flour

1 1/2 teaspoons ground ginger

1 teaspoon ground cinnamon

1 teaspoon ground allspice

1 teaspoon baking powder

1 teaspoon baking soda

1/2 cup (1 stick) unsalted butter,
    at room temperature

1/2 cup sugar

1/2 cup unsulphured molasses

1 large egg yolk

Royal Icing (recipe p.103)

101
❖

1. In a medium bowl, whisk together the flour, ginger, cinnamon, allspice, baking powder, and baking soda. Set aside.

2. In a large bowl, beat the butter and sugar with an electric mixer until light and fluffy. Beat in the molasses and then the egg yolk. On low speed, gradually beat in the flour mixture, mixing just until incorporated.

3. Divide the dough into quarters, shape into disks, and wrap in plastic. Refrigerate for at least 3 hours, or overnight.

4. Preheat the oven to 350°F.

5. Divide one of the pieces of dough in half and refrigerate the remaining pieces of dough. On a generously floured surface, roll out the dough to a 1/4-inch thickness. Cut out cookies using 3-inch cookie cutters.

Place the cookies about 1 inch apart onto ungreased baking sheets.

6. Bake for about 8 minutes, or until slightly firm.

7. Transfer the baking sheets to wire racks. With a skewer, make a hole in the top of each cookie large enough for a ribbon to fit through. Let the cookies cool on the baking sheets for 2 minutes, then transfer them to wire racks to cool completely.

8. Spoon royal icing into a pastry bag fitted with a very small plain tip. Decorate the cookies as desired. Let stand until the icing is set.

Royal Icing

Makes enough to decorate about 6 dozen cookies

❖

I large egg white
I cup confectioners' sugar plus
   additional, if needed

I teaspoon fresh lemon juice or
   1/2 teaspoon cream of tartar
Food coloring, optional

In a large bowl, beat the egg white, sugar, and lemon juice at high speed with an electric mixer for 8 minutes, or until thick enough to hold its shape, gradually adding additional sugar if needed. Beat in food color, if using. (The icing can be covered and refrigerated for up to 4 days.)

Cinnamon-Sugar Stars

These fragrant cinnamon-sugar-topped cookies make a welcome seasonal treat with a tall glass of ice-cold milk.

Makes about 5 dozen cookies

2 cups all-purpose flour
1/2 teaspoon baking powder
1 teaspoon ground cinnamon
1/4 teaspoon salt
1/2 cup (1 stick) unsalted butter,
  at room temperature
3/4 cup sugar

1 large egg
1 1/2 teaspoons vanilla extract

TOPPING
1 1/2 tablespoons sugar
1/2 teaspoon ground cinnamon
1 large egg white, beaten

104
❖

1. In a medium bowl, whisk together the flour, baking powder, cinnamon, and salt.

2. In a large bowl, beat the butter and sugar with an electric mixer until light and fluffy. Beat in the egg and the vanilla. On low speed, gradually add the flour mixture. (The dough will be somewhat crumbly.) Divide the dough into quarters, shape into disks, and wrap in plastic. Refrigerate for 2 hours, or until firm enough to roll.

3. Preheat the oven to 350°F. Grease two large baking sheets.

4. Combine the sugar and cinnamon in a small dish. Set aside.

5. On a lightly floured surface, roll out one piece of the dough at a time 1/8 inch thick. Cut out cookies using a 3-inch star-shaped cutter and place 1 inch apart onto the baking sheets. (The scraps of dough can be chilled and rerolled.) If desired, use a skewer

to make a 1/4-inch hole in the top of each cookie. Lightly brush the tops of the cookies with the egg white and sprinkle with the cinnamon sugar.

6. Bake the cookies for 8 to 10 minutes, until the edges are lightly browned. Cool on the baking sheets for 1 minute (if necessary, open up the holes with a skewer), then transfer the cookies to wire racks to cool completely.

Stained-Glass Cookies

*Make these unique cookies part of your Christmas tradition, and hang them so
the lights shine through the candy "window panes."*

Makes about 3 dozen cookies

About 10 ounces sour ball candies

3 cups all-purpose flour

1/2 teaspoon baking powder

1/2 teaspoon grated nutmeg

1/2 teaspoon salt

1 cup (2 sticks) unsalted butter,
   at room temperature

2/3 cup packed light brown sugar

1/2 cup light corn syrup

2 teaspoons vanilla extract

1. Preheat the oven to 350°F. Line baking sheets with foil and lightly grease the foil.

2. Separate the candies by color. Place each color in a resealable plastic bag, remove
the air, and seal the bags. Coarsely crush the candy with a rolling pin. Set aside.

3. In a medium bowl, whisk together the flour, baking powder, nutmeg, and salt.

4. In a large bowl, beat the butter and sugar with an electric mixer until light and fluffy.
Beat in the corn syrup and vanilla. On low speed, gradually beat in the flour mixture.

5. Divide the dough into quarters. Roll out one piece 1/4 inch thick. Using 3-inch
cutters, cut out shapes. Cut out and remove several smaller dough shapes from each
cookie; reroll. Place the cookies 2 inches apart onto the prepared baking sheets. Fill
each cutout with crushed candy. With a skewer, make a 1/4-inch hole in the top of each
cookie. Bake for 8 minutes, or until the cookies are golden and the candy is melted.

6. Let cool completely on the baking sheets set on wire racks, then peel off the foil.

107
❖

Swedish Ginger Hearts

This ginger-scented cookie is popular throughout the year in Sweden, but at Christmastime,
it is cut into holiday shapes and decoratively piped with tinted icing.

Makes about 8 dozen cookies

3 cups plus 2 tablespoons all-purpose
  flour
1 teaspoon baking soda
1 1/2 teaspoons ground ginger
1 teaspoon ground cinnamon
1/4 teaspoon ground cloves
1/2 teaspoon salt
1 cup (2 sticks) unsalted butter,
  at room temperature

1 cup granulated sugar
1 large egg
1/4 cup dark corn syrup
1 1/2 teaspoons grated orange zest

ICING
1 3/4 cups confectioners' sugar, sifted
Red food color

1. In a large bowl, whisk the flour, baking soda, ginger, cinnamon, cloves, and salt.

2. In another large bowl, beat the butter and granulated sugar with an electric mixer until light and fluffy. Beat in the egg, then beat in the corn syrup and orange zest. On low speed, gradually add the flour mixture. (The dough will be stiff.) Divide the dough into four portions, shape each piece into a disk, and wrap in plastic. Refrigerate overnight.

3. Preheat the oven to 325°F.

4. On a lightly floured surface, roll out the dough to a 1/8-inch thickness, sprinkling the work surface and rolling pin with flour as necessary. Cut out cookies using a 2 3/4- to 3-inch heart-shaped cutter. Pull away the scraps of dough from around the cutout cookies, and with a metal spatula, transfer the cookies to ungreased heavy baking sheets, placing them 1 inch apart. If you want to hang the cookies on the tree, use a skewer to make a 1/4-inch hole at the top of each cookie.

5. Bake the cookies for 9 to 11 minutes, until very lightly golden around the edges. Let the cookies cool on the baking sheets for 1 to 2 minutes (if necessary, enlarge or open up the holes with a skewer), then transfer to wire racks to cool completely.

6. In a medium bowl, combine the confectioners' sugar and just enough water to make a smooth icing that can be piped. Tint with a few drops of food color, blending well. Scrape the icing into a pastry bag fitted with a very small plain tip and pipe a thin border of icing along the edge of each cookie. Let stand until the icing is set.

Recipe INDEX

112

❖